# MEDITATIONS ON
# mid-century design
### a coloring book

by Margaret Dahm

ALL ORIGINAL DESIGNS, ILLUSTRATIONS ©2016 Margaret Dahm

*All rights reserved. No part of this book may be transmitted or reproduced by any means, photocopy, electronic, recording or any other means of information storage or retrieval, without prior written permission from the author.*

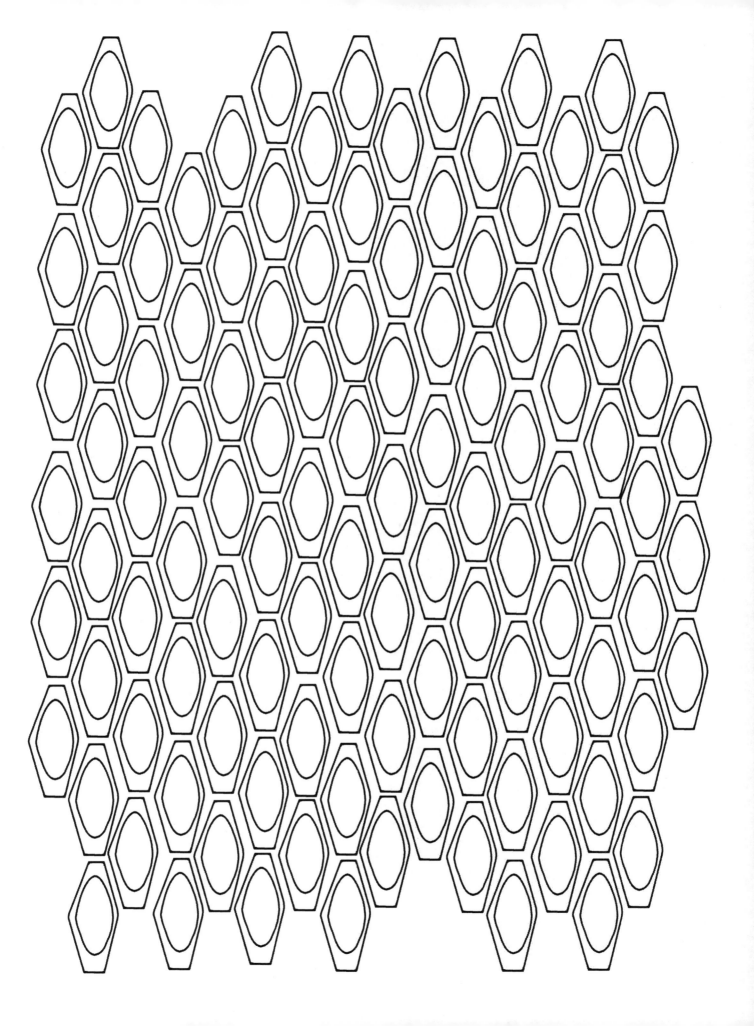

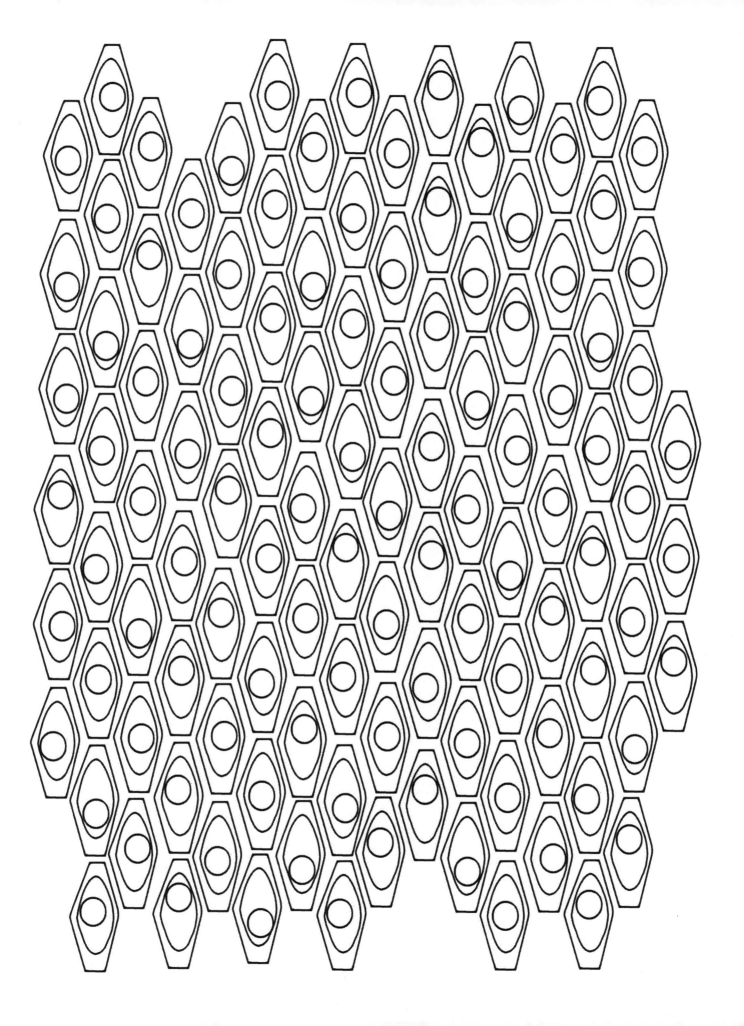

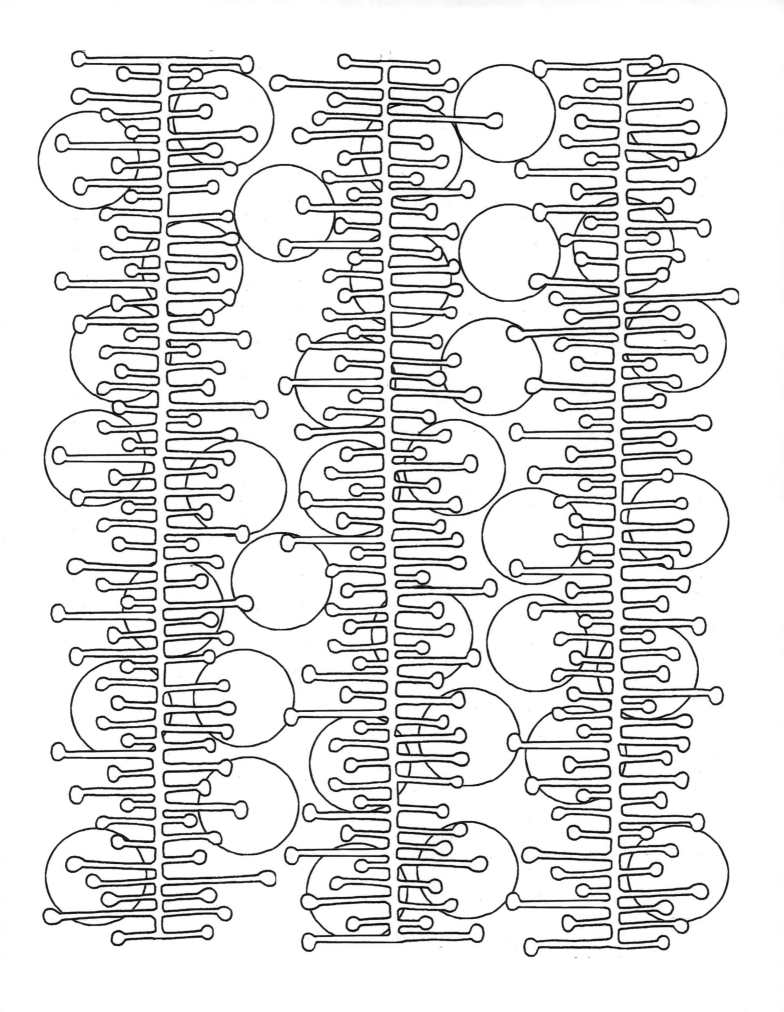

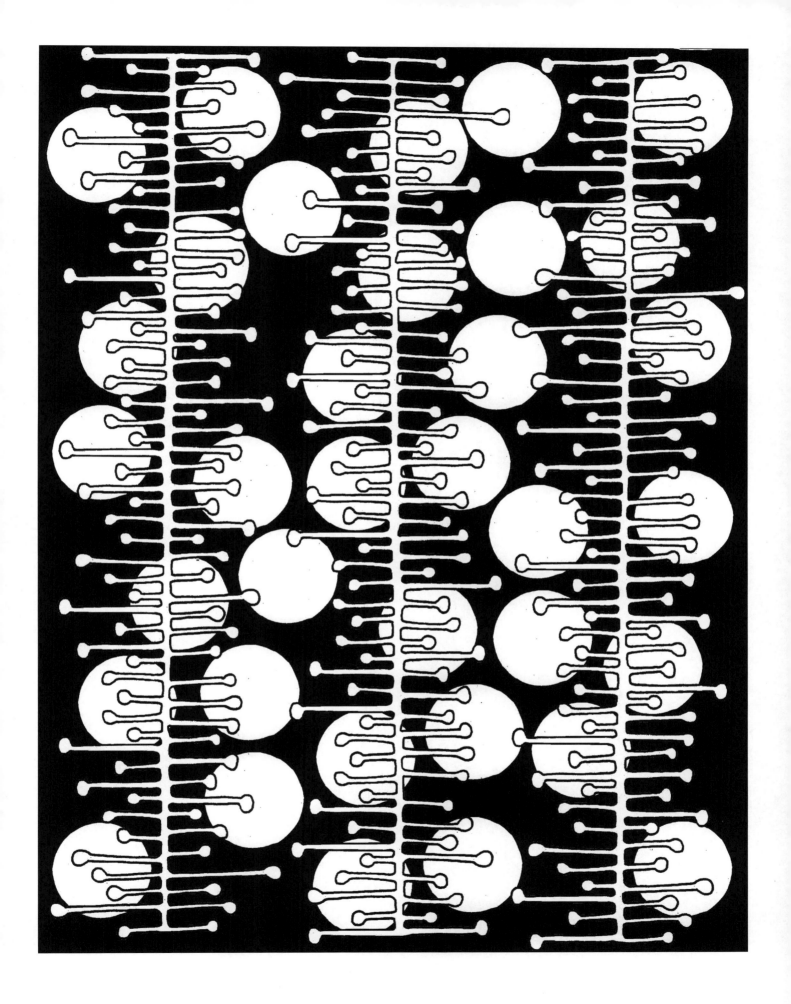

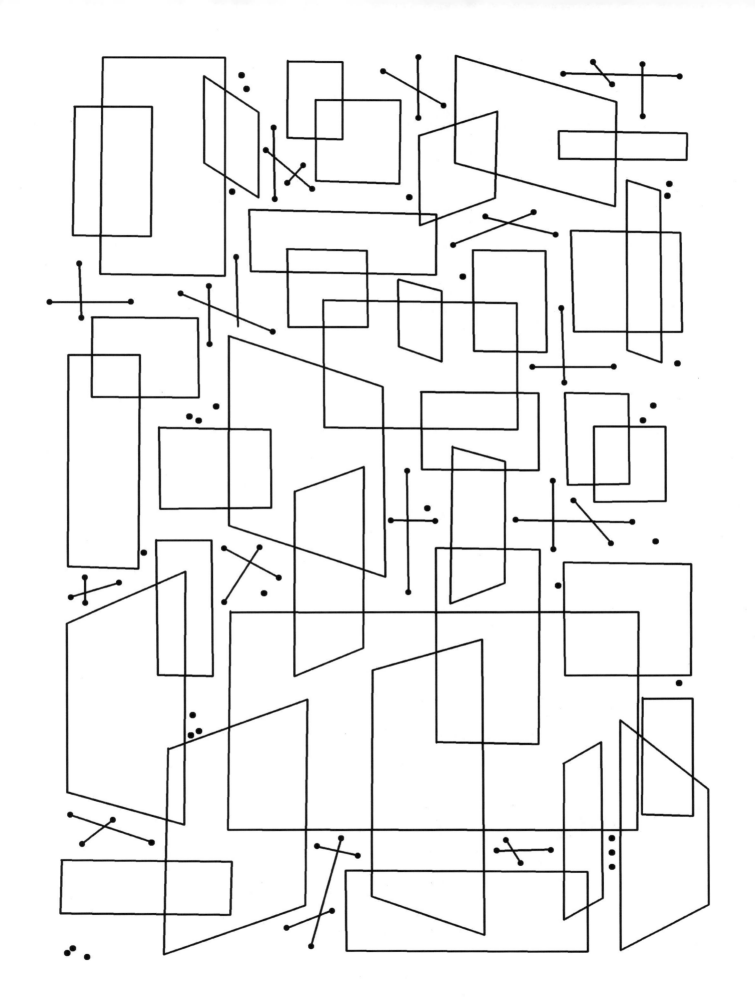

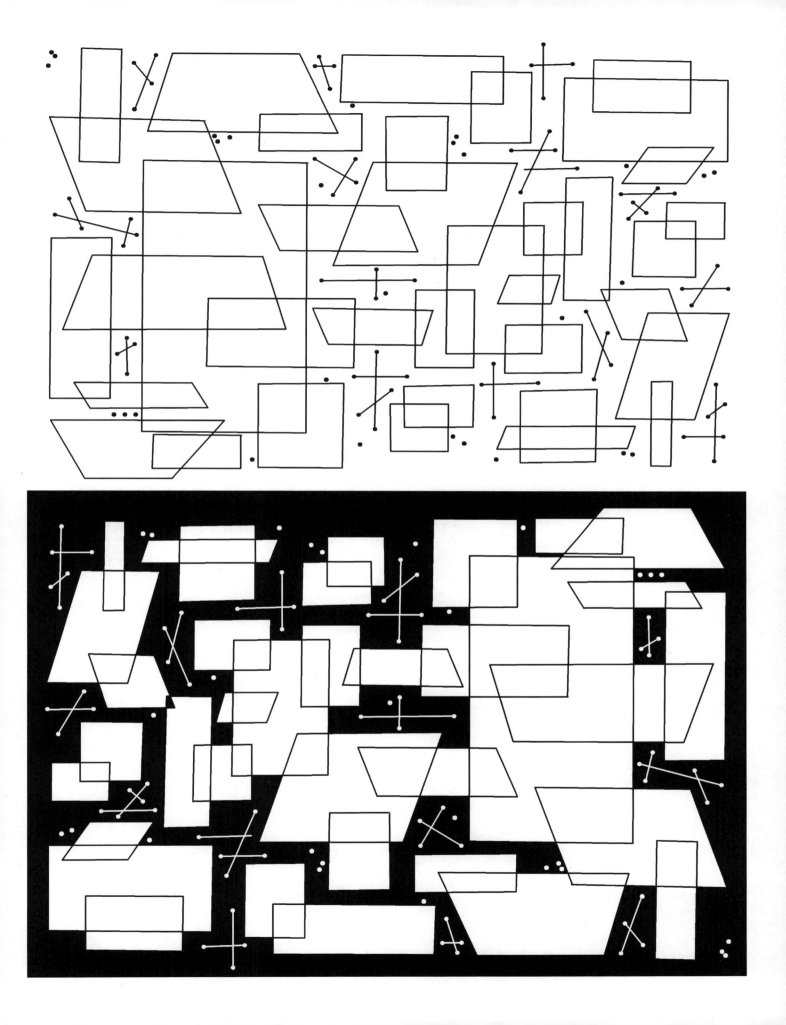

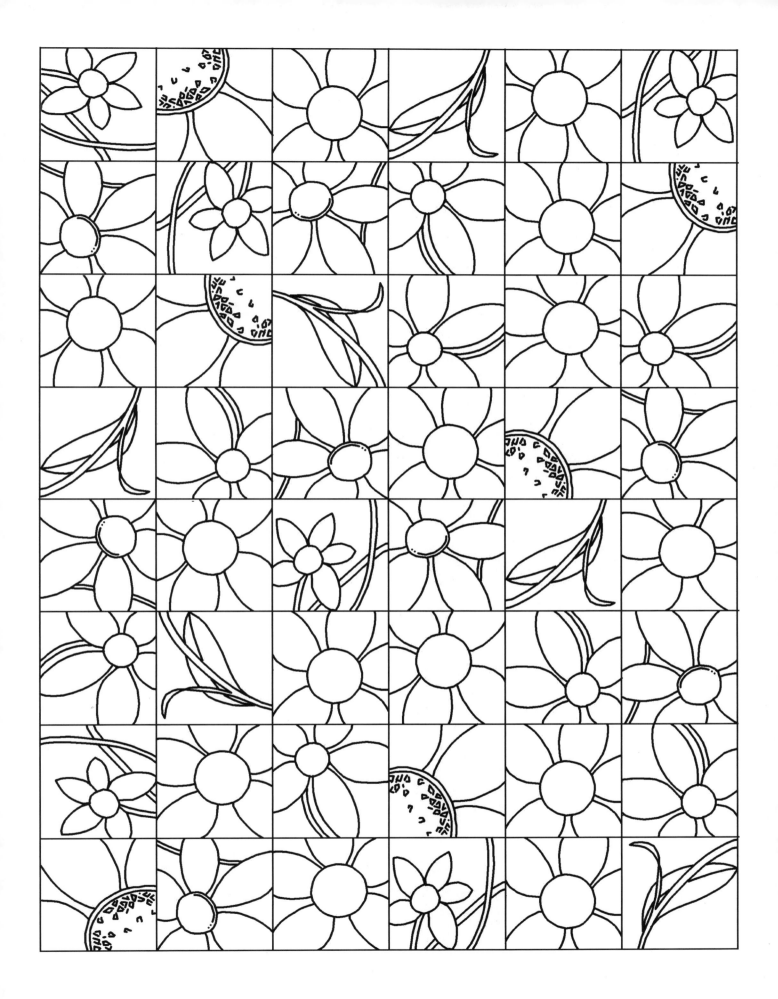

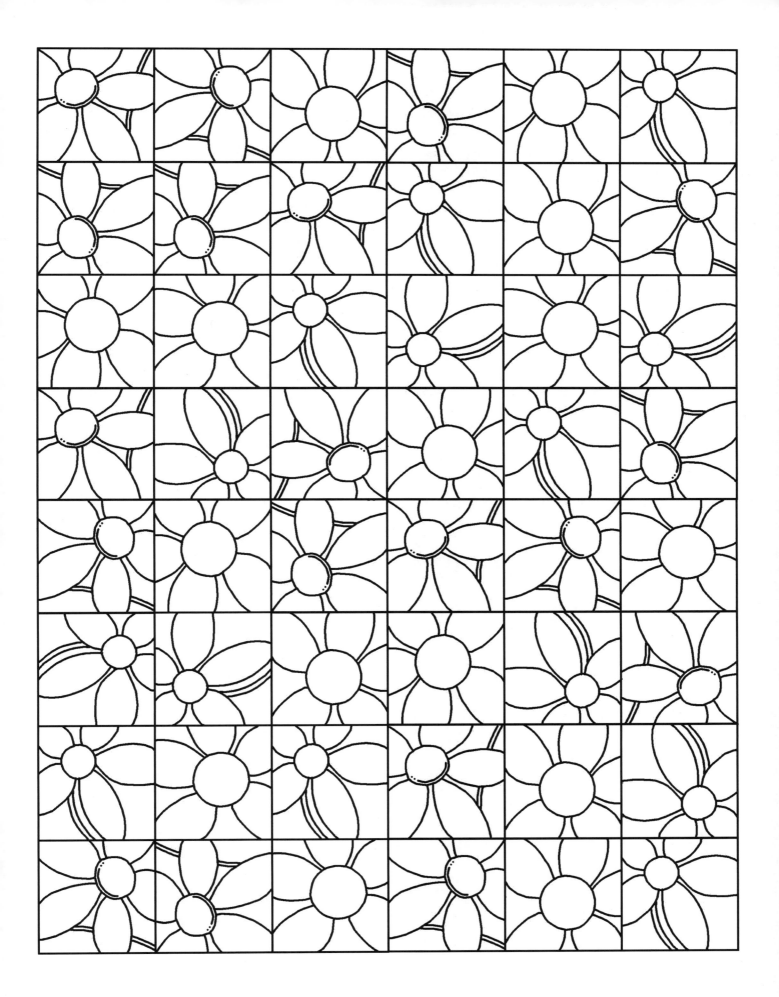

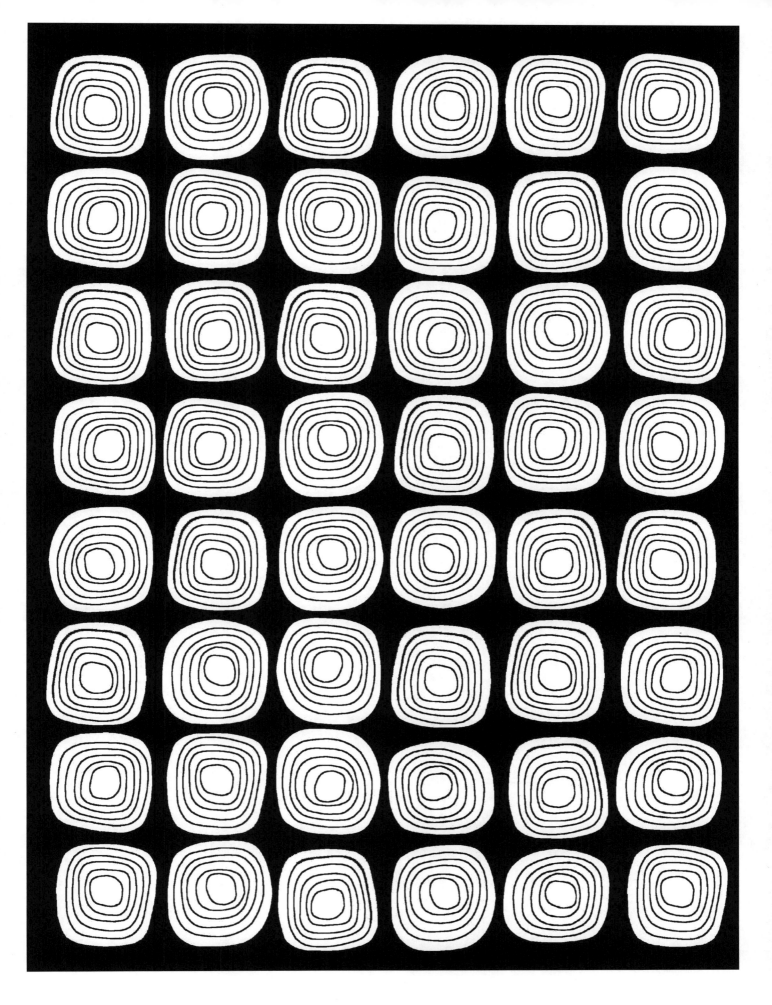

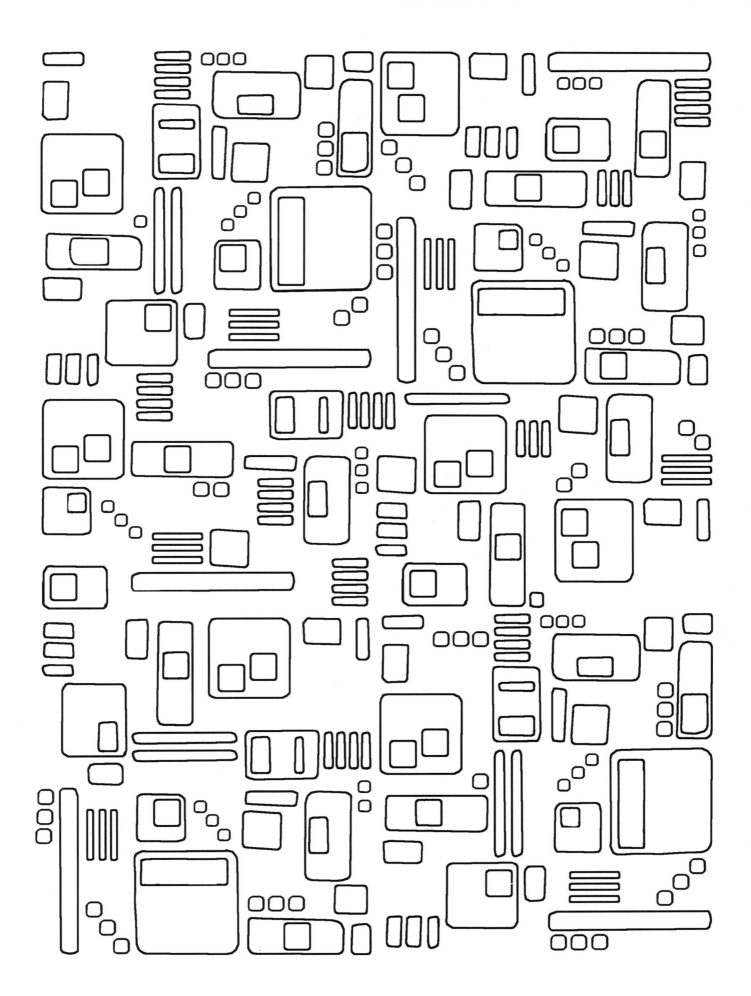

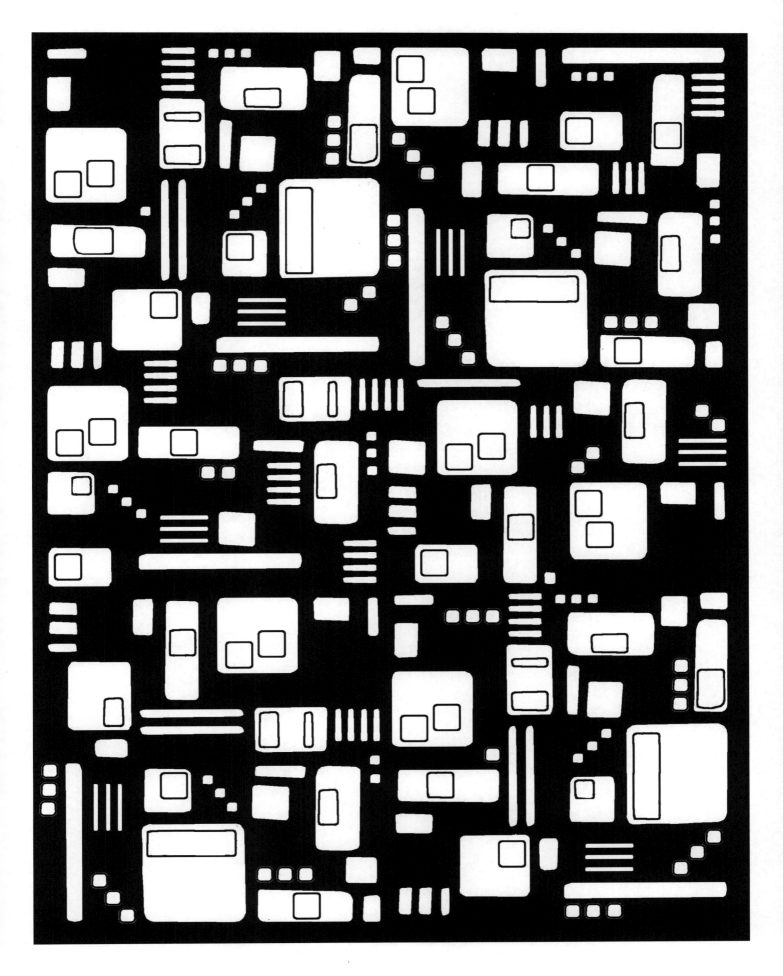

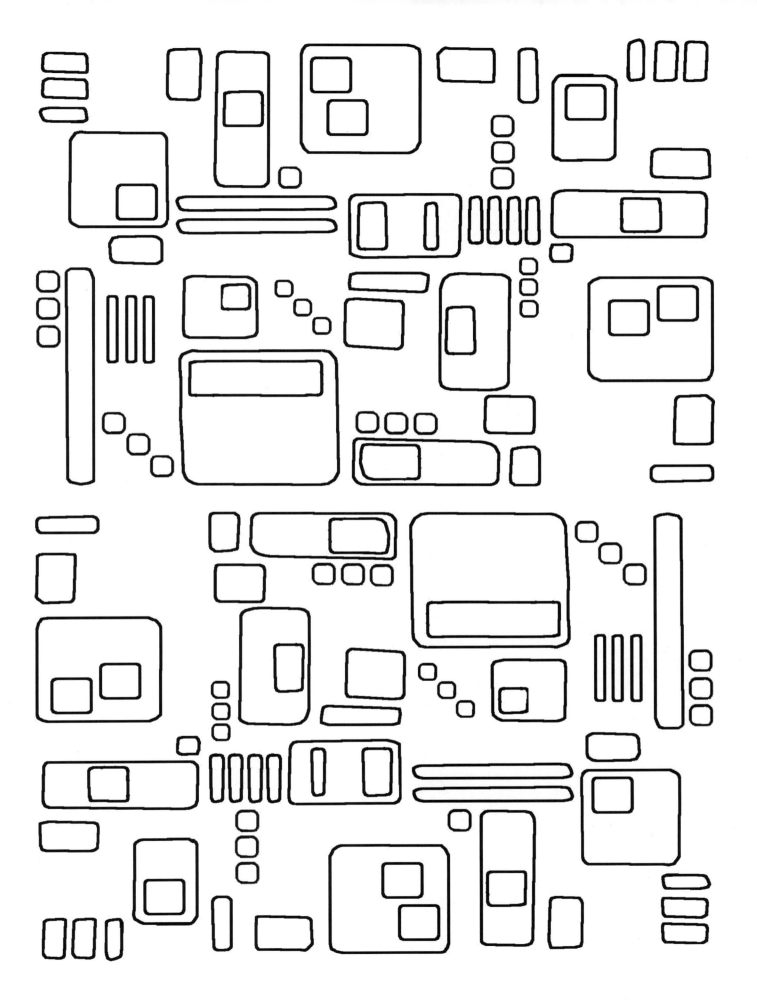

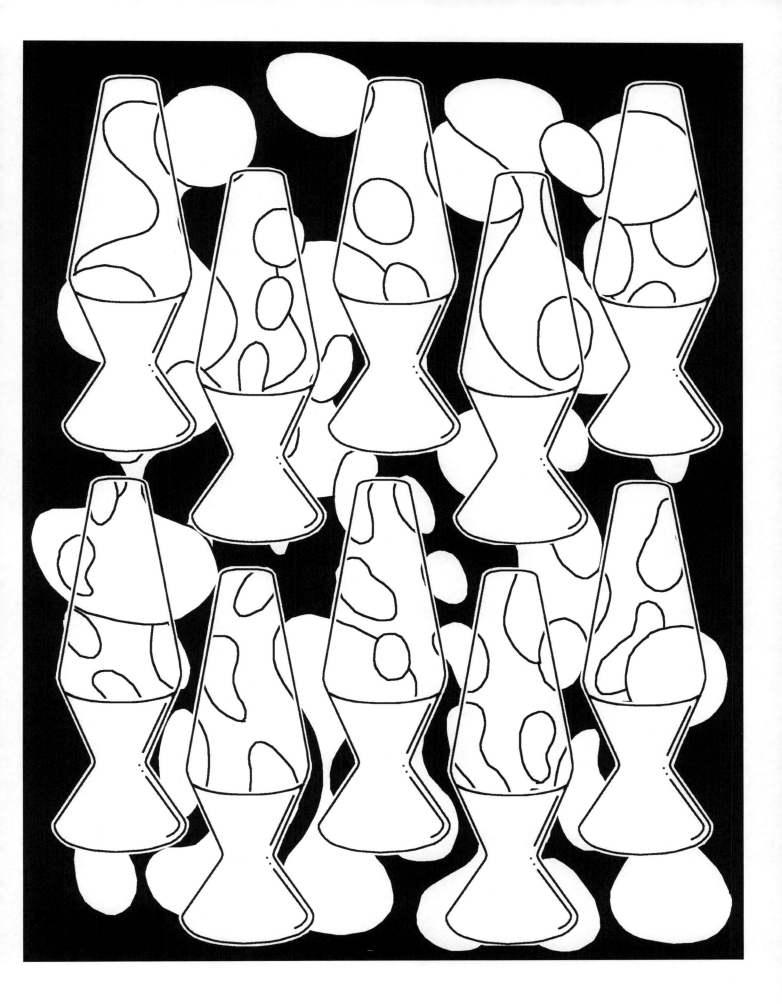

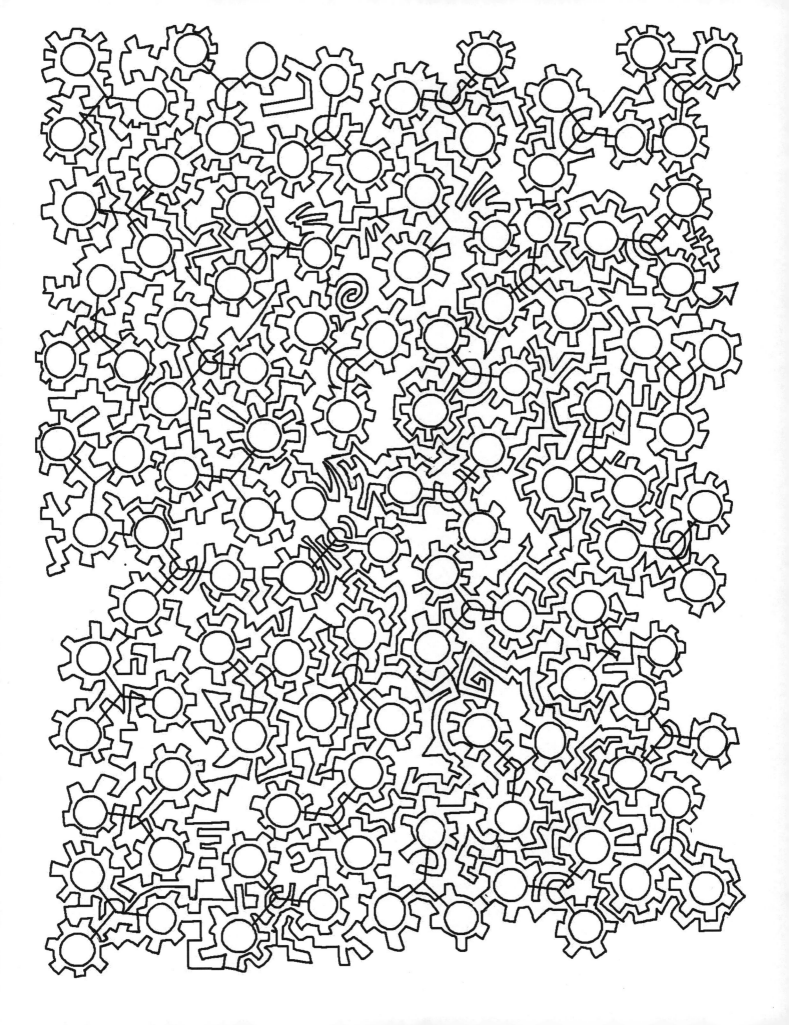

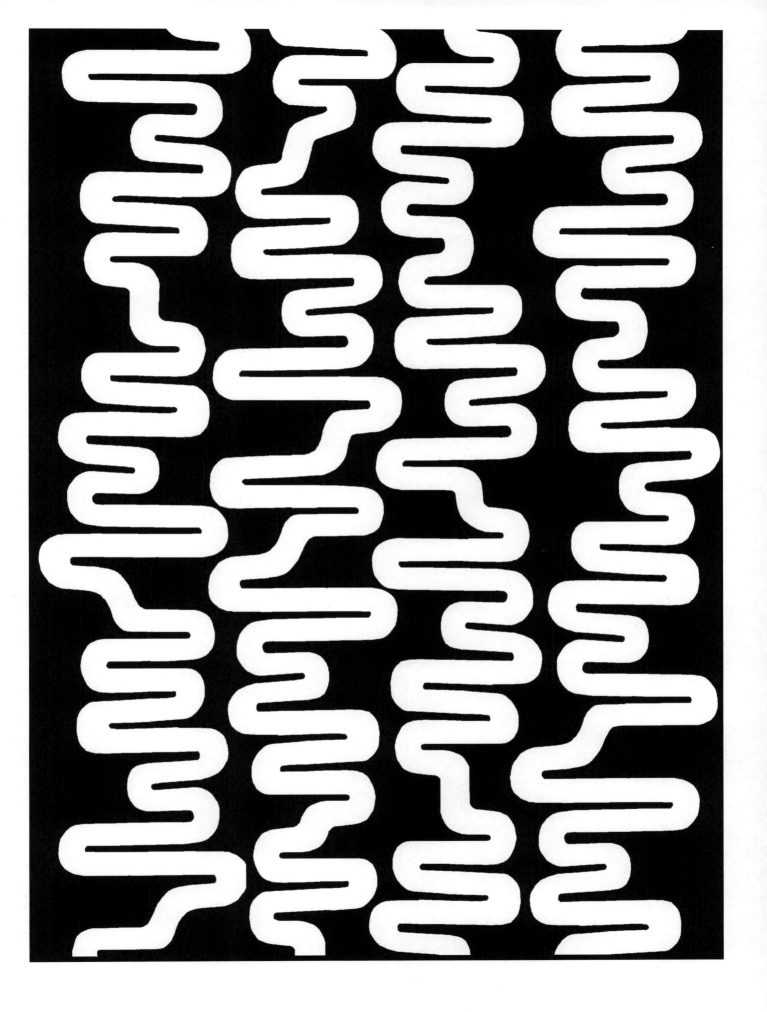

# charles + les + ray + eames

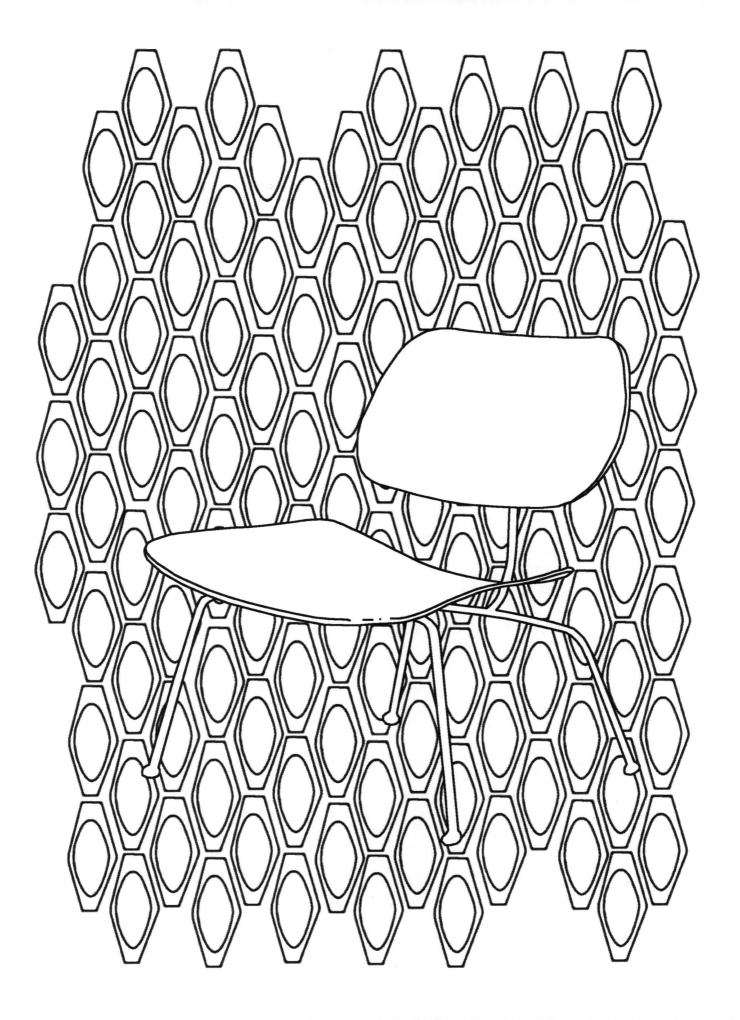

# hans wegner

# frank o. gehry

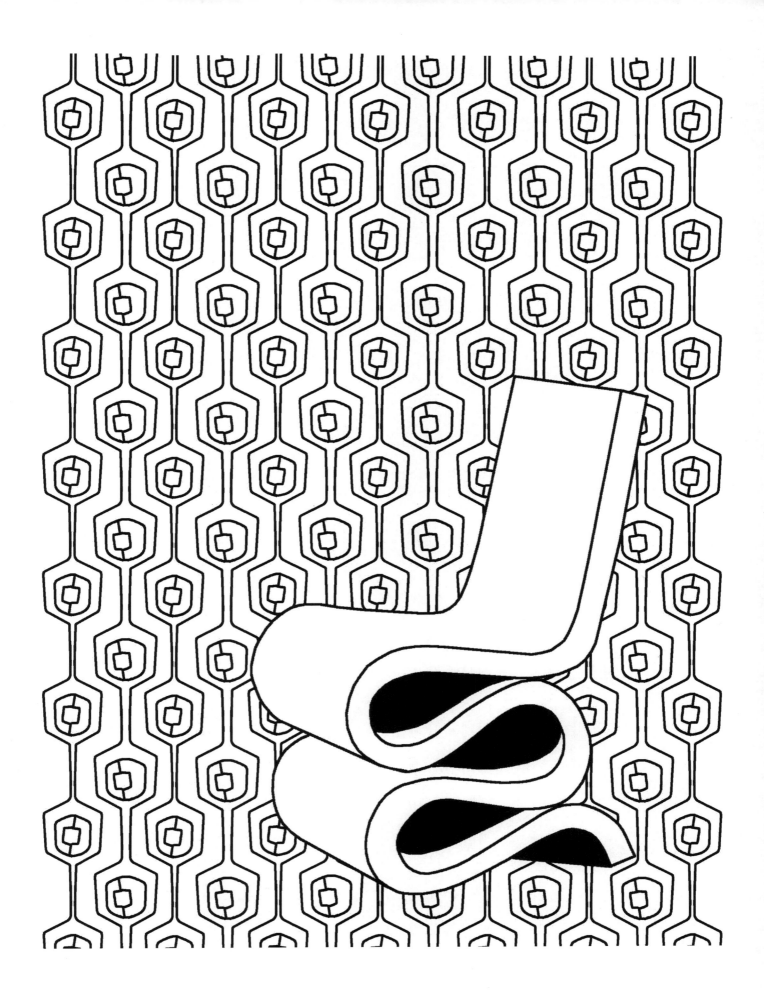

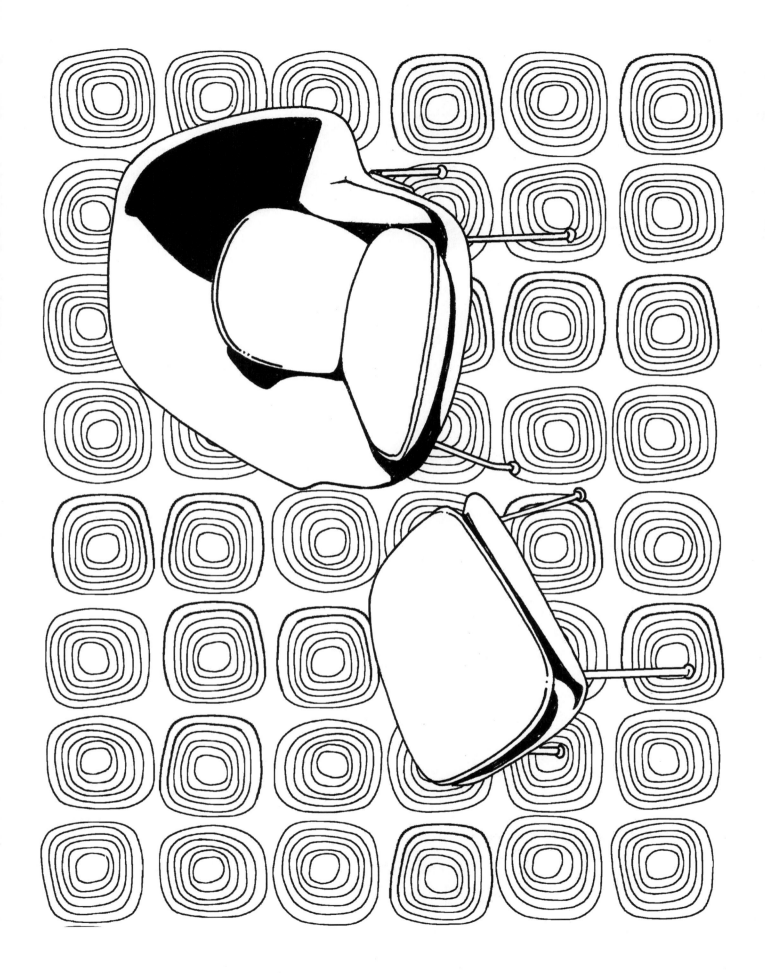

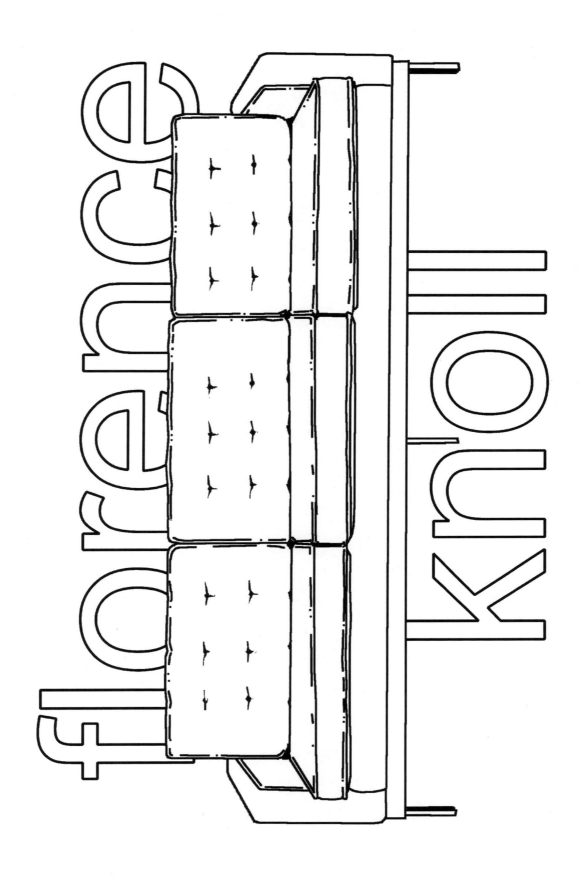

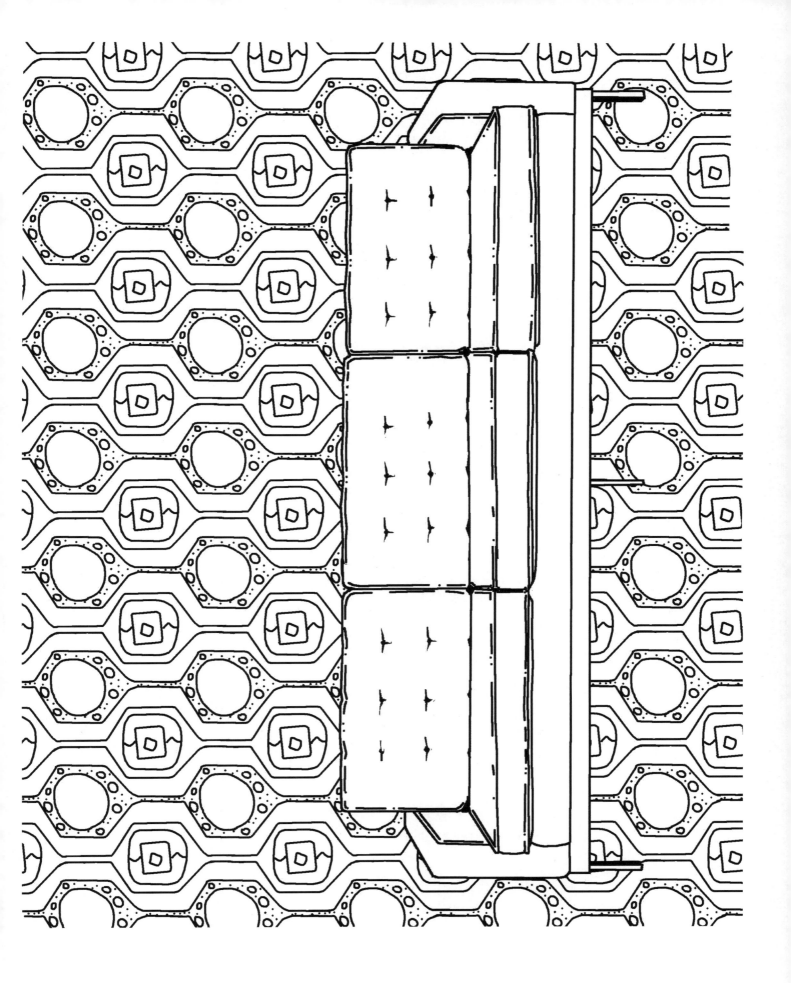

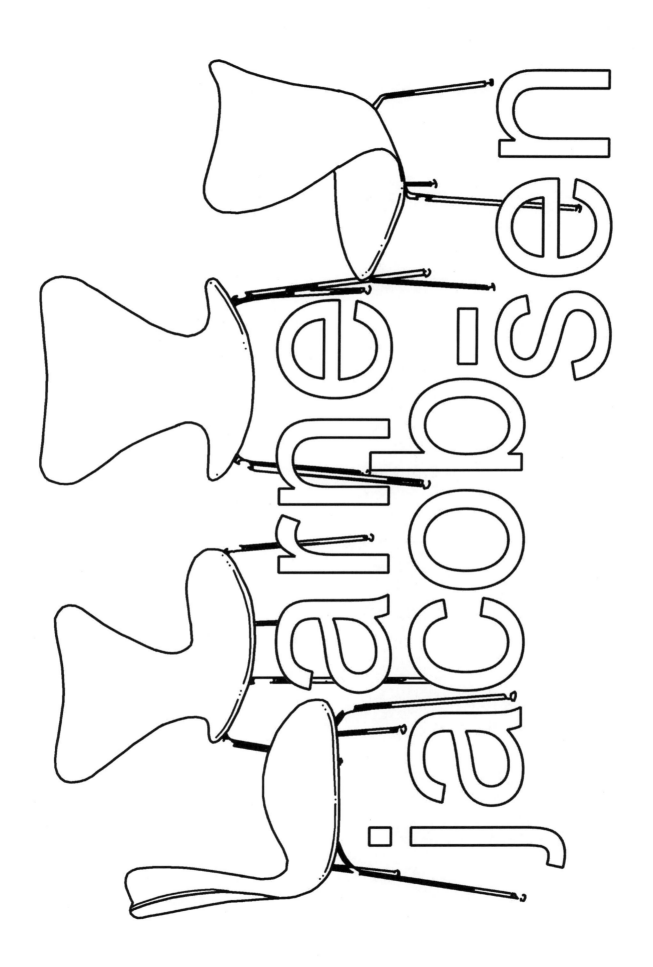

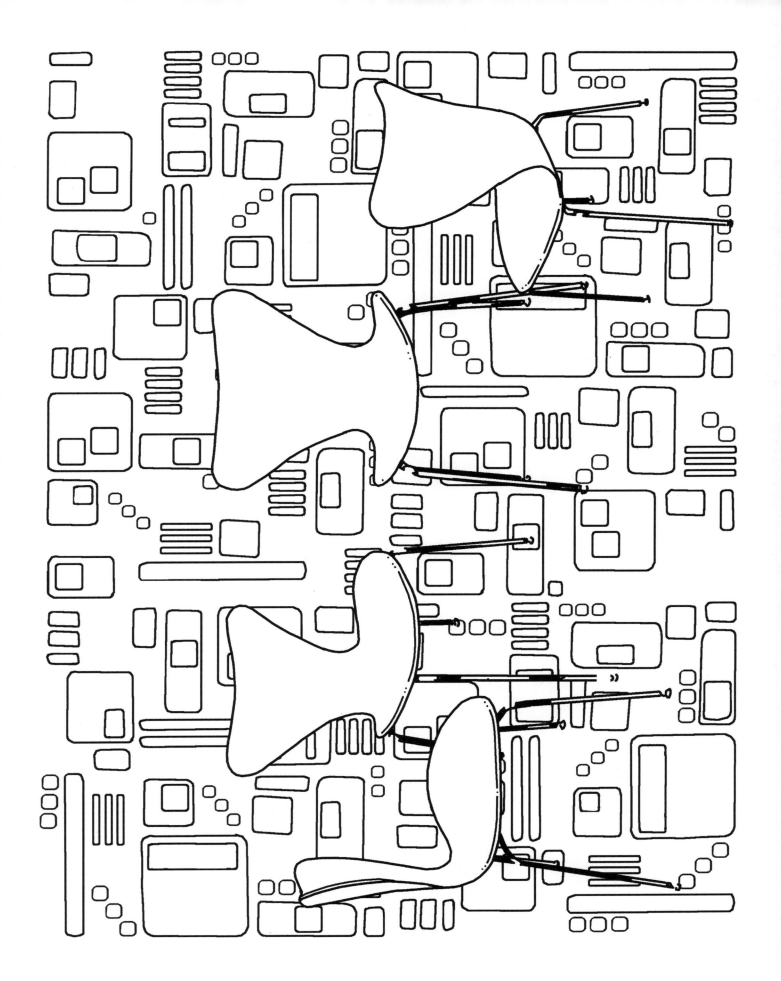

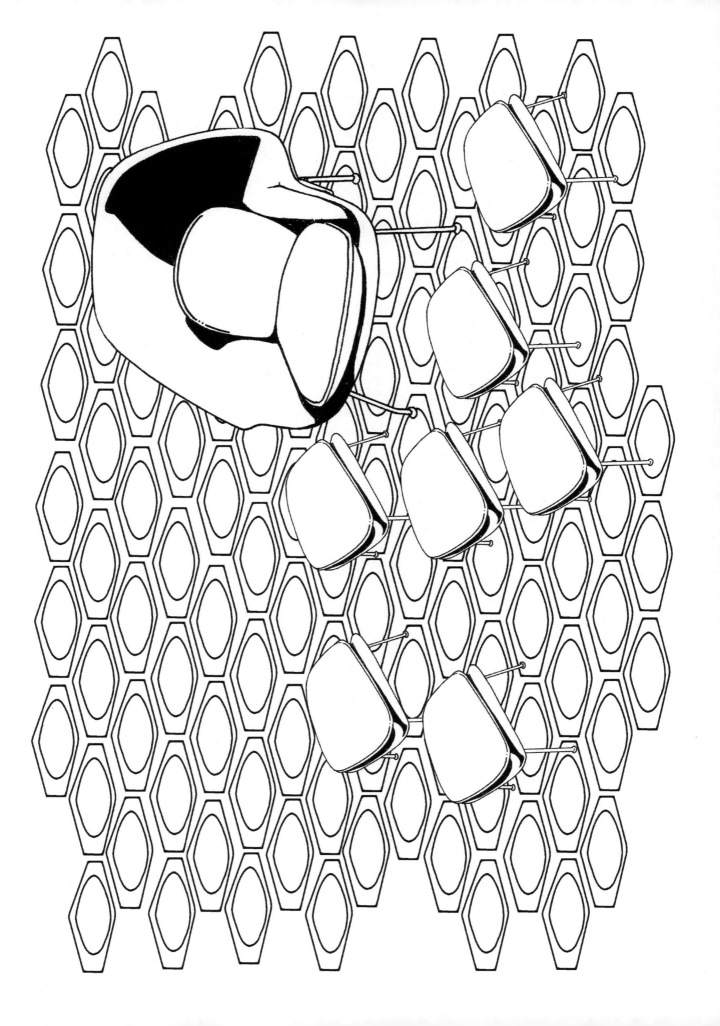

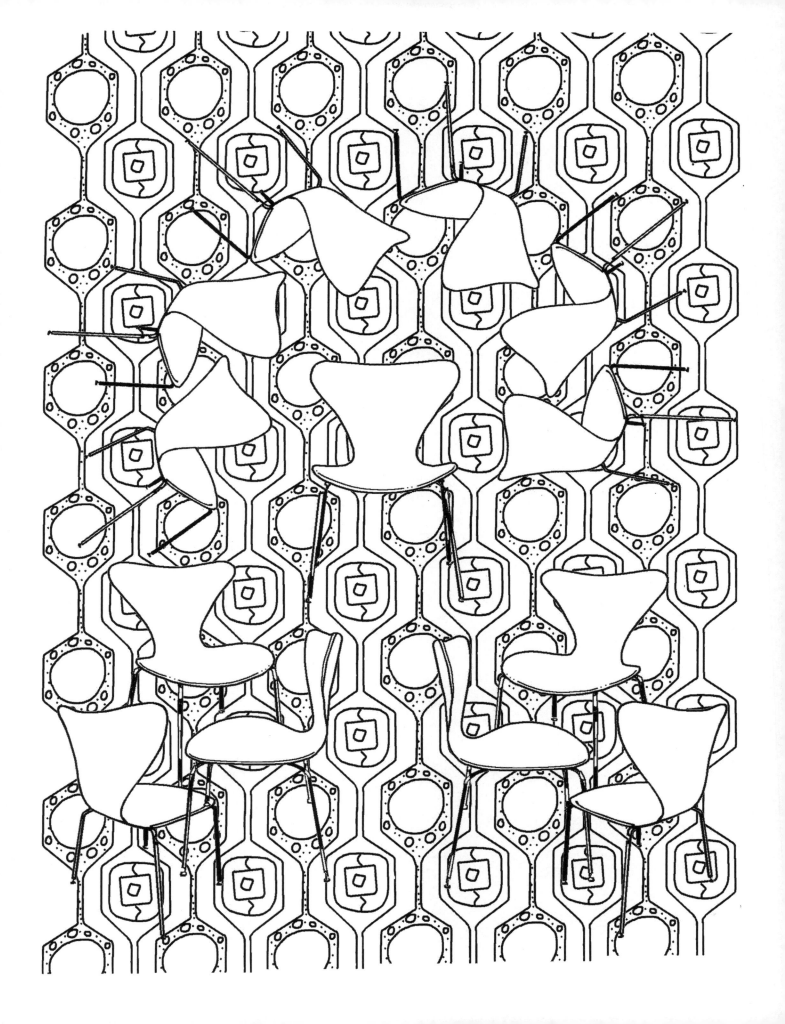

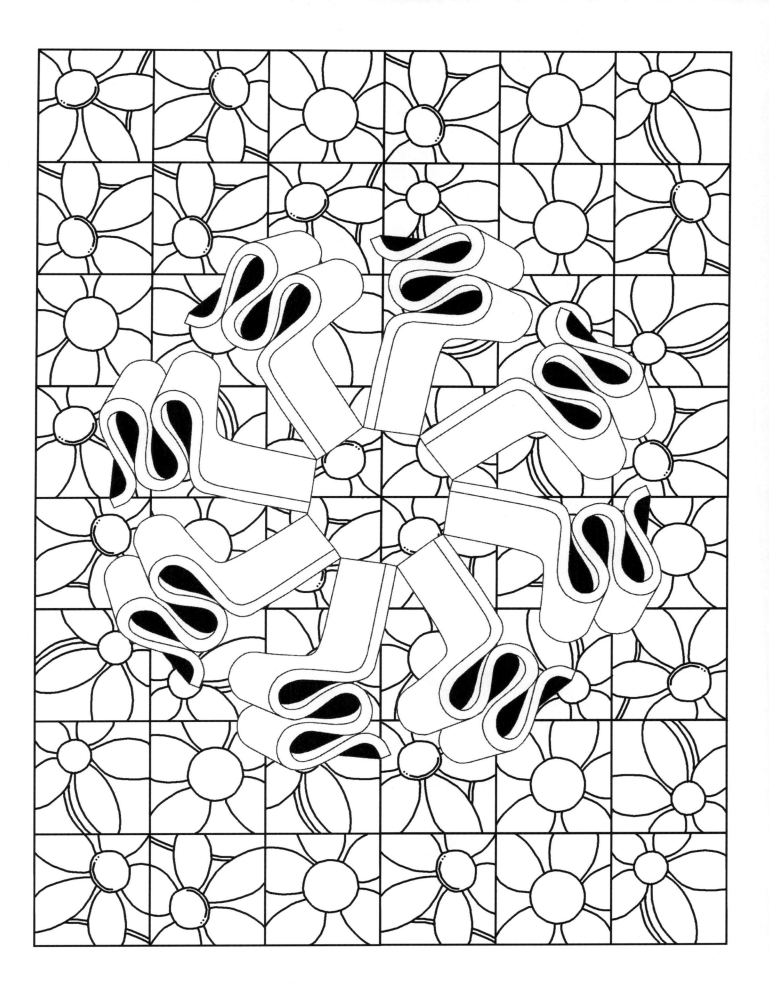

# Hope you've enjoyed your time meandering through the mid-century!

The designs in this book are all original, inspired by the unexpected patterns and unusual elements of that most fun period in pattern design.

noverso1066@gmail.com

etsy.com/shop/noverso

margaretdahm.com

The designs in this book are for personal use only.

If you are interested in licensing any of these or other designs, please contact me.

Made in United States
Orlando, FL
06 April 2023